PRIČA O BROJEVIMA

THE NUMBER STORY

SMALL BOOK ONE
ENGLISH – SERBIAN

Numbers Teach Children
Their Number Names

written and illustrated by

MISS ANNA

Early Reader Edition of *The Number Story 1*
Bronze Medal Winner, 2016 Wishing Shelf Book Award

Library of Congress Control Number: 2018902040

Names: Miss Anna, author.
Title: Number story : numbers teach children their number names / Miss Anna.
Description: Portland, OR: Lumpy Publishing, 2018.
Identifiers: ISBN 978-1-945977-49-7 | LCCN 2018902040
Summary: The pictures and rhymes present stories which introduce numbers 0-10.
Subjects: LCSH Numeration—English--Serbian--Pictorial works--Juvenile literature. | BISAC JUVENILE NONFICTION /
Languages: English--Serbian
Classification: LCC QA141.3 .M57 2018 | DDC 513—dc23

Publisher: Lumpy Publishing
Website: www.missannabooks.com
Email: missanna@missannabooks.com

Paperback: ISBN 978-1-945977-49-7
Printed in the U.S.A.   1 3 5 7 9 10 8 6 4 2

Naučite kako se
brojevi zovu,

It is very easy and a lot of fun!

vrlo je zabavno i lako!

Say-along our little jingle

Zapevajte s nama kroz pesmicu ovu!

starting from Number One!

Broj Jedan je prvi ionako!

1

ONE looks like my one finger.

JEDAN

liči na kažiprst.

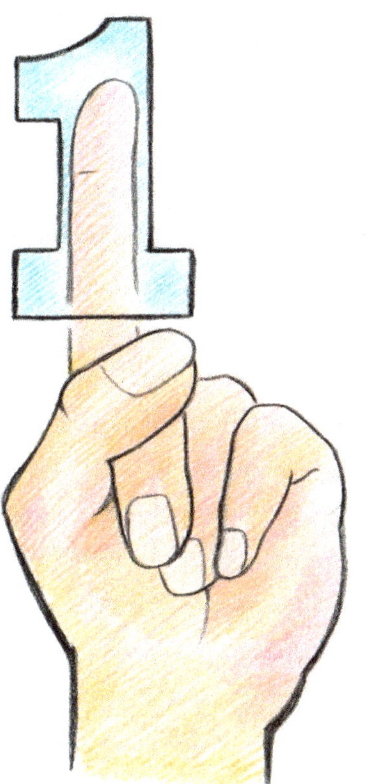

ONE!

JEDAN!

2

TWO trails a tail.

DVA

za sobom vuče rep.

A TAIL! REP!

3

THREE   has bumps.

TRI

ima čvoruge neke.

BUMPY! ČVORUGE!

4

FOUR carries a sail.

ČETIRI

jedri kroz svet.

A SAIL!
JEDRO!

5
FIVE   is a racing track.

PET

munjevito stazom juri.

VROOM
VRUM!
1

SIX   curves like a snail.

ŠEST

se uvija kao puž.

A SNAIL!   PUŽ!

7

SEVEN has a sharp angle.

SEDAM

je oštar k'o ružin grm.

OUCH!
JOJ!

8

EIGHT   is rollercoaster rails.

OSAM

je kao tobogan strm.

URA!
YIPPEE!

NINE is a bubble on a stick.

DEVET

je mehur na štapu.

A BUBBLE!   MEHUR!

10

TEN   is an eye of a whale.

DESET

je kit što mig ti šalje.

WINK!
MIG!
HELLO! ZDRAVO!

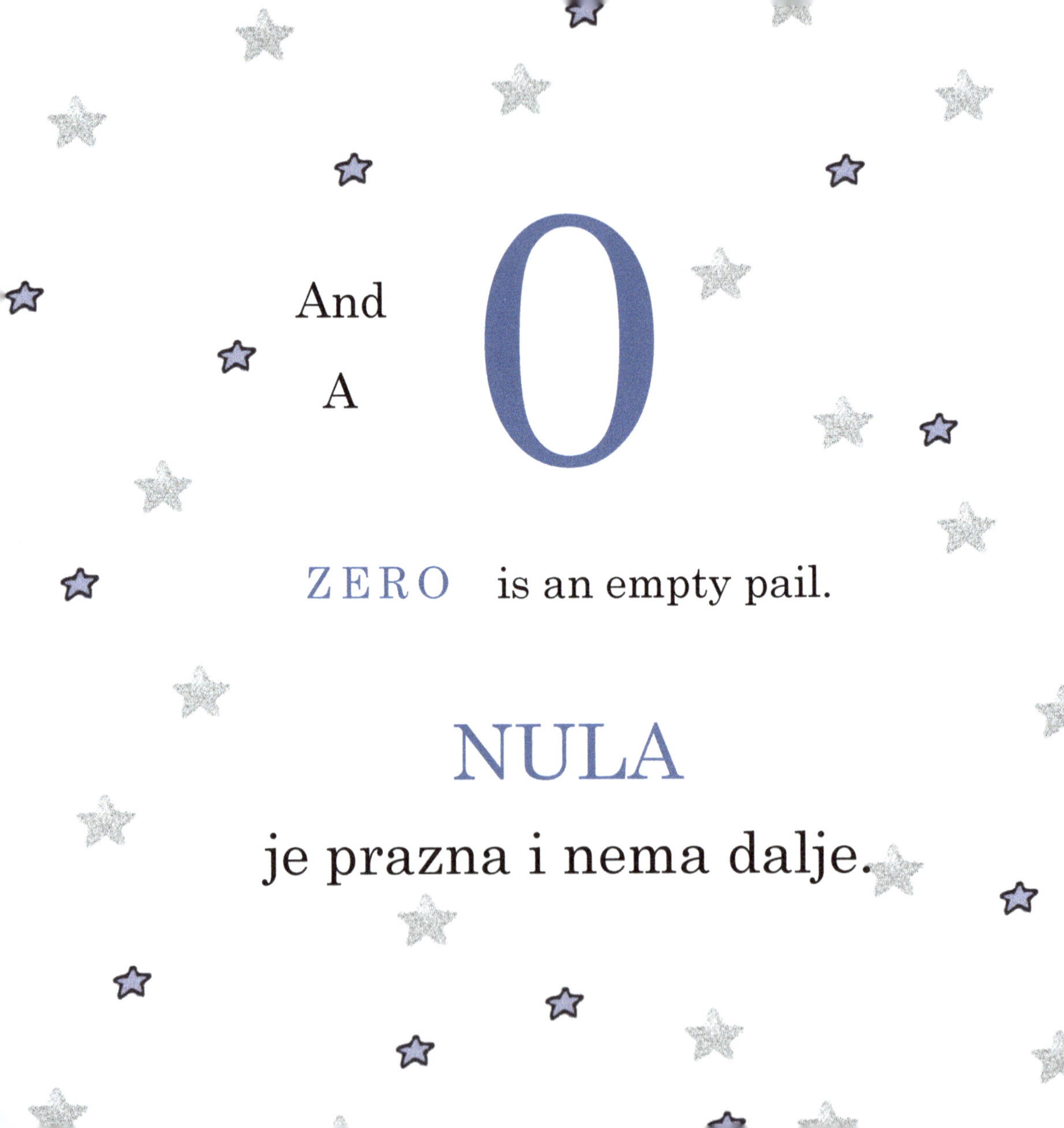

And
A
0
ZERO   is an empty pail.

NULA
je prazna i nema dalje.

IT'S EMPTY!
Prazna je!

Thank you for playing with us today.

We had a lot of fun too!

Hvala što ste se igrali s nama.

I mi smo uživali baš!

We are your Number friends,
Zero to Ten,
Who will be here for you~
**Drugari brojevi
od Nula do Deset
uvek su tu za vas!**

Bye-bye now!
See you again soon!
A sad pa-pa!
Vidimo se uskoro!

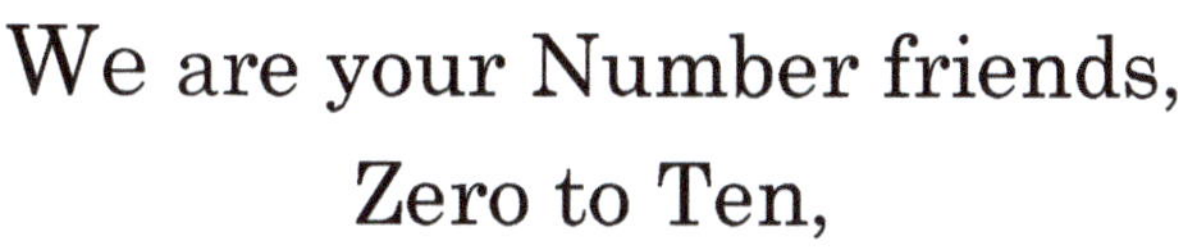

The Numbers are *SINGING* too!

To sing-a-long, look for Miss Anna Number Story
at your favorite music store like iTUNES.

MP3

Numbers 0-10
IDENTIFYING & COUNTING

Numbers 11-20
& Ordinals
first, second, third...

Numbers 0-100
& Place Values
ones, tens, hundreds...

About Clocks
& Telling Time
hours, minutes, seconds

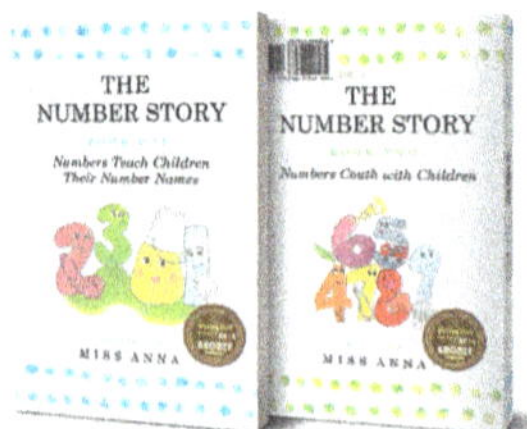

Number Story 1 & 2
isbn: 978-0-996216-48-7

Number Story 3 & 4
isbn: 978-1-945977-01-5

Number Story 5 & 6
isbn: 978-1-945977-06-0

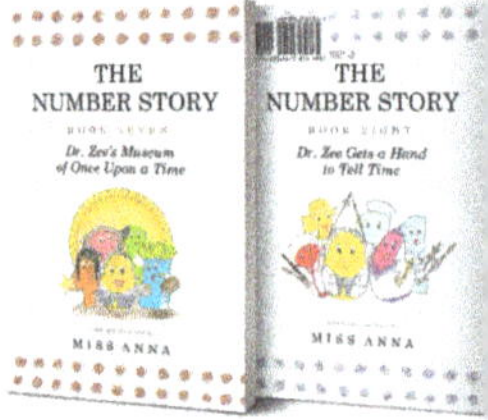

Number Story 7 & 8
isbn: 978-1-949320-40-4

For more Miss Anna books to love,
visit us at

www.missannabooks.com

Numbers are working hard all over the world!
Come Travel the World with Us!